Once upon a time there were the Romans

Elisabetta Siggia

PALOMBI EDITORI

© 2005
All rights to
Palombi &Partner
Via Timavo, 12
00195 Roma

Designed and edited by
Palombi Editori

Art director
Ugo Bevilacqua

Drawings
Elisabetta Siggia

Translation by
Isobel Butters Caleffi

ISBN 88-7621-406-2

Printed in February 2005
by Palombi & Partner, Rome

The origins of the Romans date back to the 8th century BC when an Italic tribe of Latins settled in the central Italian area now called Lazio. The Latins were farmers who lived in the hills. They were always fighting with the neighbouring tribes, especially the Sabines and the Etruscans. A legend says that Rome first grew up on the Palatine hill and then developed on six other hills: the Quirinal, Esquiline, Viminal, Caelian, Capitoline and Aventine.

So Rome became the city of the seven hills, which were then inhabited by surrounding tribes.

The populations that inhabited the hills were often at war with each other, but in time their common needs united them and in the end they all merged together in one single big city.

Rome was founded in 753 BC. Legend says that Romulus, son of the god Mars and Rhea Silvia was its first king and also its founder. He was followed by six more kings: Numa Pompilius, Tullius Ostilius, Ancus Martius, Tarquinius Priscus, Servius Tullius and Tarquinius Superbus.

At the height of its splendour Rome had about one million inhabitants and large numbers of temples, sanctuaries, theatres and public buildings.

Goddess Roma

Capitoline she-wolf

Tarquinius Superbus, the last king, was a tyrannical ruler who aroused hatred and resentment. The Roman people rebelled and the Tarquinius family was forced to flee. In 509 BC a new type of government known as a republic was introduced. Under the monarchy all the power was in the hands of the king: he was head of the army, the most important priest, supreme judge and administrator of all the nation's wealth. Under the republic, on the other hand, legislative bodies and the judiciary kept one another in check. The republic was led by two consuls elected annually by the assembly of citizens, but it was the *senators* who took the most important decisions. The *dictators* held power only at times of war; the *praetors* made sure justice was respected and they presided over the courts; the *censors* kept the register with the citizens' wealth. They decided the taxes to be paid, and watched over the morals of the citizens; the *quaestors* were in charge of State finances; the *aediles* were responsible for public works, roads, bridges and aqueducts and they took charge of their upkeep; the *tribunes* protected the interests of the plebeians, who were the poorest members of the public; the *pontifex* was responsible for overseeing the worshipping of the gods. As time passed, the privileged classes and the judiciary became corrupt. The people, who were by now discontented, placed the task of governing in the hands of a single emperor.

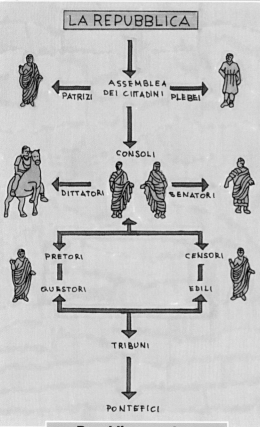

LA REPUBBLICA

PATRIZI — ASSEMBLEA DEI CITADINI — PLEBEI

CONSOLI

DITTATORI — SENATORI

PRETORI   CENSORI

QUESTORI   EDILI

TRIBUNI

PONTEFICI

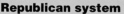

Republican system

IN the 3rd century BC the most powerful cities in the Mediterranean were Rome and Carthage.

Through maritime commerce Carthage, founded by the Phoenicians, had conquered the supremacy of the Mediterranean. After occupying most of Italy, the Romans decided to extend their conquests to the Mediterranean. The first war between Carthage and Rome started in 264 BC and lasted 23 years. To fight the Carthaginian fleet the Romans built 120 ships and later another 200. The Romans won, chased the Carthaginians out of Sicily, conquered Sardinia and Corsica and proved to be unbeatable. Two more wars followed this one and the three wars were called the *Punic* wars because the Carthaginians were also known as *Poeni*.

Carthage then turned its attention to Spain, which it conquered. With their newfound strength the Carthaginians crossed the Roman borders, and in 219 BC the second Punic war began; this lasted 17 years. Hannibal the Carthaginian, leading an army of 40,000 men and 37 elephants, crossed the Alps and after various battles defeated the Romans at Cannae. Rome chose Publius Cornelius Scipione to lead its army, and he succeeded in defeating Hannibal and his army at Zama. Carthage was forced to hand Spain over but, despite defeat, it refused to accept the laws of Rome. In 149 BC the third Punic war began: three years later the Romans had conquered Carthage and its territories had become a Roman province named Africa.

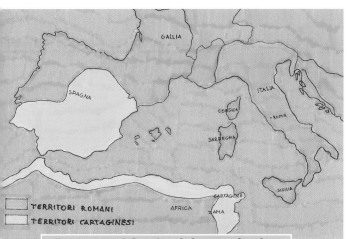

TERRITORI ROMANI
TERRITORI CARTAGINESI

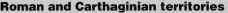

Roman and Carthaginian territories

Fighting elephant with seat for driver

Julius Caesar was a very clever politician with brilliant military skills: his victory in battle made him extremely popular, and this allowed him to march on Rome against his rival Pompeius. Caesar beat Pompeius in numerous battles and he became a dictator for the rest of his life.

On 15 March 44 BC, Julius Caesar was stabbed to death by a group of conspirers in the Senate Curia.

After Caesar's death his adopted son, Caius Octavianus, and his friend Marcus Antonius (Mark Anthony) enjoyed great power. Both wished to rule and decided to share the Roman world out between them: Octavianus took the lands in the West and Marcus Antonius those to the East. Antonius settled in Alexandria and married Cleopatra, Queen of Egypt. However, neither the Senate nor Octavianus could allow the Roman state to be divided, and in 32 BC they declared war on Cleopatra and, therefore, on Antonius.

Octavianus defeated Antonius at Azio in Greece after a long and bloody naval battle. A few months later, Octavianus conquered Alexandria and, rather than fall into his hands, Anthony and Cleopatra killed themselves. In 31 BC Octavianus became sole ruler of Rome and in 27 BC the Senate awarded him full powers. Octavianus proclaimed himself emperor and was given the name Augustus, meaning *divine*.

The Roman Empire lasted until 476 BC.

During this time it was governed by a succession of supreme chiefs known as *emperors*. Octavianus was considered a good emperor, but some of those that followed him were mad and wasted the funds of the State.

The Senate confer to the Emperor the title of "Augustus"

Expansion of the Roman empire

Emperor Augustus

Julius Caesar

Often a senator chosen by the emperor was given command of the legions. Beneath him were the *tribunes* and a *prefect* or field commander. Each legion was made up of *cohorts*, subdivided into *centuries* led by centurions, who were special soldiers chosen for their courage and valour. Their task was to train the soldiers to fight and to teach them discipline. The legionnaires had a bronze helmet, chain mail armour, a shield, a sword, and a dagger, a saw, a pickaxe, a scythe and some cooking tools.

Permanent camps were erected near the borders of the Empire. These camps were usually rectangular and were surrounded by massive walls with sturdy gates and tall towers used as lookouts against the enemy. In the centre of the camp were the headquarters and accommodation for the officers, while the soldiers' lodgings were lined up around the walls. Small villages grew up outside the walls. The centre of social life was the market around which shops, inns and taverns soon appeared. There were even schools and hospitals. In time these villages developed into real cities.

The Romans were skilled fighters on land, but not so well organised at sea until 264 BC, when they were forced to face the powerful warships of Carthage.

At this point they decided to build their own fleet. In a short space of time they built 150 ships, copying a Carthaginian ship that had fallen into their hands. After this, Rome too became a sea power.

Merchant ship "Oneraria"

Roman camp

War ship "Trireme"

Roman society was divided into three classes: patricians, cavaliers and plebeians. The patricians were part of the aristocracy and had full powers and great privileges. The cavaliers – merchants, provincial governors, prefects and praetorians – had large fortunes. The largest group was made up of the plebeians. They did not have a lot of power, but their Assemblies were important in influencing the approval of laws. They worked as teachers, doctors, architects and traders.

There was also a great number of slaves, who were mostly prisoners of war. Some were deserters or debtors and they had no legal rights. The slaves did all kinds of work: they were servants in private homes, they worked in the countryside or were employed for public works, such as the construction of roads, aqueducts and buildings.

The better educated ones served their masters as secretaries or accounts clerks. A master could free his own slave, who would then become a freeman. *Freedmen* could have their own businesses and manage their own earnings. During the imperial age freedmen were even given State jobs.

The family played a very important role in Roman society: the man was the head, and the wife and children had to show devotion and obedience. Although women were expected to obey their husbands, they were held in great consideration. Children were brought up to respect their country, their religion, laws and traditions.

At 17 a boy officially became an adult; he wore the white *toga virile* like all Roman citizens and he earned the right to take part in public life.

Bronze plate with inscrition by a "freedman"

Slave at the market

Rome's town planning scheme began to change when Augustus came to power. He reorganised the city by dividing it into 14 districts, which were subdivided into quarters governed by two *curatores urbani*. One of the most impressive works built during his empire was the Forum, a large square protected by a high wall made of blocks of stone that enclosed public buildings and temples.

The construction work in the town planning scheme continued during the reign of other emperors as well: Agrippa rebuilt the sewers and widened the roads; in 118 AD Hadrian built the Pantheon, "temple of all the gods"; Vespasian began building the Colosseum, which was completed by Titus in 80 AD. The Colosseum was so called because of its size, although there is also a theory that there was a colossal statue of Nero nearby. Roman engineers and architects were highly skilled. The cities had structures and services to suit the needs of their inhabitants. The aqueducts carried water through channels that originated at the source of a river and brought the water right to the city. Lead pipes ran underground, bringing water to the fountains, houses and thermal baths. If the aqueducts had to cross a low area of land, a brick conduit supported on arches was built. The first Roman aqueduct was constructed by Appius Claudius in 312 BC and the first one on arches was the 81 km-long Acqua Marcia (144 BC).

Roads connected the provinces, and so encouraged economic, political and military relations. These roads were wide and paved, with milestones that indicated the distances and marked every mile. Triumphal arches were erected to commemorate the emperors' victories. The oldest road is the Appian Way, built in 312 BC.

Arch of Titus

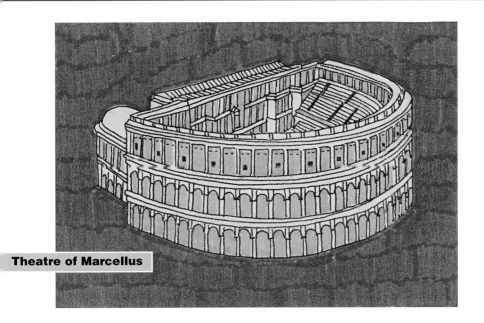

Theatre of Marcellus

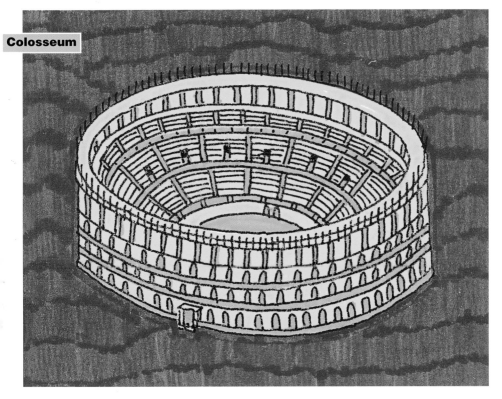

Colosseum

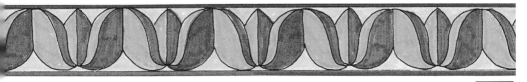

In ancient Rome a lot of plebeians lived without jobs. They received a card called an *Annona* from the State, and this enabled them to support their family.

The patricians, on the other hand, were given land by the State in recognition for their military undertakings.

Many citizens were doctors, engineers and architects. The most prestigious careers were those of politicians, military men and lawyers. However, there were also painters, sculptors, musicians, manufacturers, craftsmen and traders.

Rome's streets were filled with shops: anyone with initiative could open one. Some products were imported from the East, from Greece, Arabia, Spain, Egypt, Gallia, Phoenicia; while others came from farms or the surrounding countryside.

In daytime the streets in the centre were crowded with people browsing and shopping, attracted by the cries of the hawkers and their wares. In certain areas the shops that sold the same kinds of article gave their name to the street itself, like Sandal Makers' Lane or Spice Lane. There were silversmiths, jewellers, blacksmiths, glassmakers, farriers, carpenters, furniture makers and many others.

In the taverns people drank cups of warm wine flavoured with spices, but you could also eat focaccia (flat bread),and sweets made of flour, honey, cheese and cooked grape must.

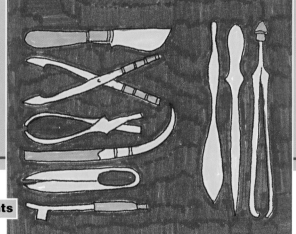

Surgical instruments

Blacksmith's forge

Butcher's shop

Chemist's shop

At first, the Roman theatre was influenced by Greek theatre both in its architecture and its performances.

The Roman theatre was a semi-circumference divided in two parts, one for the stands where the people sat and the other for the stage.

The emperor and his court sat in the imperial box, next to which were the stands for the priests, nobility and the vestal virgins. It was not necessary to buy a ticket because the costs were paid by the State.

The public was very noisy and shouted at the actors all the time, but everyone seemed to have a good time.

'Mimes' were very popular – these were imitations of important figures or animals, and they alternated with dances and singing; then there were 'pantomimes', which acted out fables or traditional legends.

The Romans' admiration for the Greek world extended to the figurative arts: the wealthiest families brought artists from Greece to decorate their homes with frescoes and mosaics.

The artists showed their clients a catalogue with the works they could execute and the subjects chosen were then represented on the walls either by fresco or mosaics. Mosaics were used for the floors: pieces of stone cut into small squares were laid down next to one another and were fixed together with mortar.

The subjects were mythology, epics, or landscapes with floral decorations.

Mask for a tragedy

Theatre mask

Musician with spiral horn

Actor playing

Musician and dancer

Until the 2nd century BC parents taught their children: the mother was responsible for teaching them good manners and the father taught them to read and write, but also horse riding, fighting, swimming, and to respect the laws of the State. As their wealth increased, families began to send their children to private teachers.

Children went to school in small groups from the age of seven. The lessons, held by the *magister ludi*, started very early in the morning and ended in the early afternoon.

The school year started in March after the feast of Minerva, goddess of knowledge, and continued all year without any summer holidays. The children of the more well-off families studied at home with a tutor, who was often a *freedman*.

The secondary school teacher was called a *grammaticus.* The children learned the works of the Latin and Greek poets, history, geometry, arithmetic, geography, music and astronomy.

At the age of 17, the patrician and wealthier families sent their children to Greece to continue their studies with *rhetors*, from whom they learnt the art of oratory, which would help them aspire to political posts or the legal profession.

Students used two different instruments for writing: wooden boards coated in wax that were engraved on with a wooden, metal or bone pen, or else sheets of parchment or papyrus, which they wrote on us-

ing thin canes dipped in ink. Books were copied by slaves. The increase in the number of books led to the establishment of real libraries, where books could be consulted and read.

Writing tools

Girl with pen and tablet

Originally the Romans worshipped the *numina*, invisible spirits that governed all natural events. The *Lares*, guardians of the family, and *Penates*, guardians of the economy and the State, were the spirits of their ancestors. After this, the Romans adopted the Greek divinities, who had the appearance of humans.

The most venerated were: Jupiter, god of the sky and father of all the gods; Juno, female protector of women, marriage and birth; Mars, god of war, also considered to be the father of Romulus; Mercury, protector of merchants and travellers and messenger of the gods; Apollo, god of beauty and protector of the arts; Neptune, god of the sea; Venus, goddess of love, and many others. As the empire expanded, new faiths were introduced from the East and new gods took hold, such as Isis, Mytra and Cybele. Even the emperors were worshipped as gods by the Romans.

They honoured their gods with prayers, offerings – generally fruit, milk, honey and wine – and sacrifices. Animals were covered with wine in a special ritual and then sacrificed on the altar.

A white bull was given in sacrifice to Jupiter, a horse to Neptune, doves to Venus, while only black animals were sacrificed to the evil gods.

The Romans also believed in the art of divining, and interpreted the flight of birds, thunder and lightning, while the *haruspex* and *augurs*, who were priests that foretold the future, examined the entrails of sacrificed animals, believing they could interpret the wishes of the gods.

When Christianity, which allowed only one God, gained ground the Romans refused to consider the emperor a divinity.

The Christians were persecuted for three centuries because of this refusal. In 312 AD, the emperor Constantine finally made Christianity the State religion.

Emperor Costantine

The god Mytra sacrificing a bull

At home the Romans dressed simply and comfortably: on top of their underwear they wore a sleeveless woollen, linen or silk tunic which reached the knees and was kept in at the waist by a belt. Their footwear consisted of sandals or slippers. When they went out they wore a toga and leather footwear with leather soles.

The toga was a sign that the person was a Roman citizen and it was considered a mark of distinction. It was made up of a rectangle of soft cloth without stitching or fastening and it was passed over the shoulders and under the arms in ample drapes. In cold weather the men wore a type of tight leather trousers, called *bracea*, which came down to the ankles.

Women wore a linen or silk tunic, which was longer than the men's; on top of this they wore a *stola*, another, wider, cotton or silk tunic, tightened at the waist with a belt. When they went out they covered themselves with a wide shawl, called a *palla*, which was draped over the head.

Both men and women wore hooded cloaks knotted or fastened with a brooch at the neck.

The women liked to be in fashion and spent a lot of their time putting on make up. They used a great many creams and perfumes and took great care over their hair. Hairstyling took a long time and sometimes the hair was kept tidy in a fine net or with a hairpin.

It was also fashionable to dye the hair, and the most popular colours were blond and red. Wigs too were much in use; these were usually made from the hair of captives. Both men and women wore a lot of jewellery: brooches, rings, earrings, necklaces and hairpins were most popular.

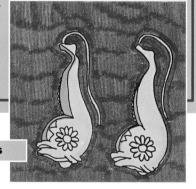

Gold dolphin earrings

Roman matron

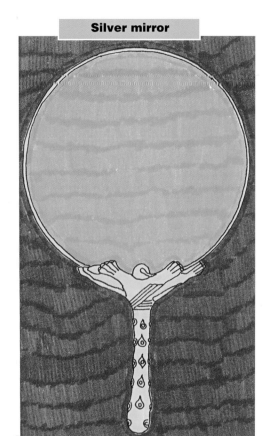

Silver mirror

Ivory comb

The Roman Empire stretched from Britannia to Africa, from Spain to Mesopotamia and it was along these routes that a lively trade started. Goods were transported by ship, carts or camels and some items, such as grain, gold, silver, lead, tin and iron were controlled by the Roman State. Often the citizens' need was greater than production.

For example, every year over 500,000 tons of grain were imported from Egypt and North Africa. Luxury items were also traded: linen, silk, pearls, spices, perfumes and marble. Even entertainment played its part.

Every year bears were brought from Britannia, elephants from India and crocodiles from Egypt. Rome exported as well as imported many products including wine, oil, pottery, *garum* and dried fruit. Food was shipped in amphorae, which were large terracotta jars.

Roma was the centre of commerce with the Mediterranean cities.

Trade took place mostly by ship, as this was the fastest and least expensive way. The ships left from and arrived at the ports of Civitavecchia, Brindisi, Pozzuoli and Ostia. The port of Ostia stood at the mouth of the Tiber, about 20 km from Rome; this is where the import-export companies had their warehouses.

They advertised their products with a mosaic picture on the ground outside.

At first the Romans used animals for barter. Afterwards metal coins were introduced.

Anphora used for trade

Transportation ship

Mosaic floor in shop at port of Ostia

In ancient Rome, public buildings constructed especially for entertainment were very important and the circus was one of the most popular buildings. The biggest was the Circus Maximus, 600 metres long by 200 wide. It stood between the Palatine and Aventine hills.

Various different types of competition took place in the circus, such as gladiator fighting. Gladiators were usually prisoners of war turned slaves. They were very well trained and very fit and they fought to the death. Some fought with weapons and had a shield and armour. The gladiators paraded in front of the spectators. They stopped in front of the emperor's box to pay him homage. Then the trumpet sounded and the games began. The fighting was extremely violent and the men alternated with wild and exotic animals, including panthers, lions, boars, hyenas, elephants and others. You could also watch simulated fights at the circus, or acrobatics on horseback, jumping competitions or chariot races, which were hugely popular. The chariots – pulled by between two and ten horses with precious harnesses – were flimsy and very dangerous to drive, especially when curving. The race consisted in completing the greatest number of laps around a track split down the middle by a barrier known as a *spina*. There were a lot of accidents and the driver, called a *charioteer*, was often fatally wounded even though he wore a bronze helmet. The winner was fêted with songs and dances that continued late into the night, and he was rewarded with fame and riches.

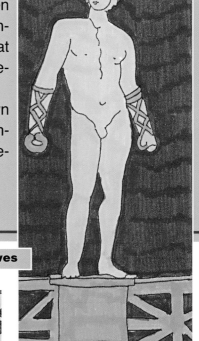

Also very popular were naval battles known as *naumachia*, which were held in the amphitheatre arena, flooded with water especially for the occasion.

Boxer wearing gloves

Picture of a naumachia

"Paegnarii" jesting fighters

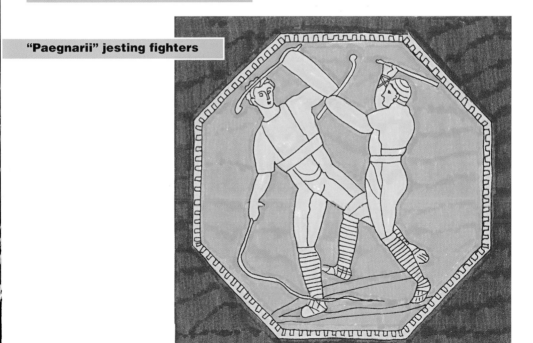

Initially the staple foods of the Romans were spelt, barley and wheat. These cereals were used to make "farinata", a sort of polenta, or maize porridge, flavoured with oregano, mint or rosemary dressed with oil. This was served with meat, fish, vegetables, olives or cheese.

The Romans also ate large quantities of apples, pears, cherries, grapes, figs, almonds and chestnuts. Bread appeared later: the most common was white bread, eaten mostly by the rich, and black bread called *plebeius*. Meat – boiled, roasted, spiced or served with a sauce – was mostly for special occasions but, as living standards improved, it became part of the daily diet.

A much appreciated sauce was *garum*, made with salted fish fermented in the sun.

The Romans ate three meals a day: breakfast (*ientaculum*) consisted of bread with honey or cheese, eggs or fruit; lunch (*prandium*), which was eaten around midday, was very quick and included cold meat, fish, vegetables, bread and fruit, all accompanied with honeyed or spiced wine, sometimes served boiling hot. Supper (*coena*) was the main meal of the day: it started at dusk and was eaten lying on special beds laid out in a horseshoe around the table. There was a starter of eggs, fish and vegetables; sometimes oysters and snails were served in milk, or else there were stuffed dormice, all accompanied by a mixture of watered down wine sweetened with honey.

Dishes of boiled, roasted or stewed meats followed, and the meal ended with fruit and sweets; then the toasts started and the dancers, actors and musicians appeared. The Romans also liked fish, poultry, game, venison, stork, mutton and ostrich. The food of the poor was simpler and less varied, but even with little money you could go to an inn and eat hot food served with wine.

Food products

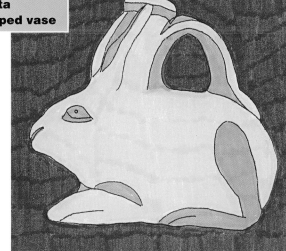

**Terracotta
hare-shaped vase**

In the 2nd century AD the Roman empire reached its maximum expansion, and this was one of the reasons for its downfall. The emperors, often inept, were unable to single-handedly govern such a vast territory, which was increasingly threatened by barbarian invasions. In the 3rd century the political and economic crisis was so severe that emperor Diocletian divided it into two parts: West and East. Constantine moved the capital to Byzantium (Constantinople). On the death of Theodosius the empire was divided up between his sons: Honorius was given the West with Rome as its capital and Arcadius the East, with Byzantium as the capital.

The Empire was never reunited again, and the two empires were often at war with each other.

The Western Empire lasted less than a century, and its territories soon fell into the hands of the barbarians. The last Western Roman emperor was Romulus Augustulus, who reigned from 475 to 476 AD. Rome was sacked by Visigoths and Vandals, and in 476 AD a Goth named Odoacre, proclaimed himself king of Italy. Emperor Justinian re-conquered the lands taken away by the Vandals, the Ostrogoths and Visigoths and tried in vain to reunite the Empire.

Portrait of emperor Justinian

The Eastern empire, less besieged by barbarians, continued to prosper and was governed by Christian emperors. In 1453 Constantinople fell under the dominion of the Ottoman Turks.

Portrait of emperor Theodosius

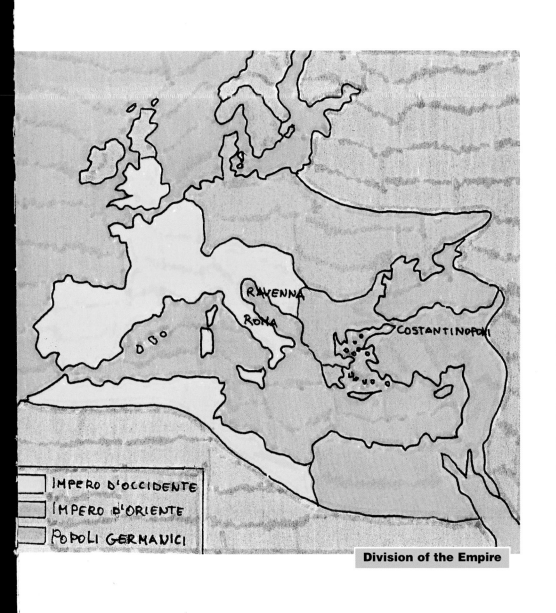

RAVENNA

ROMA

COSTANTINOPOLI

IMPERO D'OCCIDENTE

IMPERO D'ORIENTE

POPOLI GERMANICI

Division of the Empire

PALOMBI EDITORI

ISBN 88-7621-406-2

Euro 5,00